Hope Beyond Defeat

Hope Beyond Defeat

MYRA WOODBRIDGE

WRITER'S TORCH
Press & Media

Writers Torch LLC
1795 Alysheba Way, Suite 7203
Lexington, KY 40509
Phone Number: 347-768-7550

Copyright © 2025 by Myra Woodbridge

ISBN 979-8-89175-183-5 (sc)

DEDICATION

To all those who Terry and I call *our*
friends and our loved ones:
We love you and hold you dear to our hearts always.
We dedicate this book to you.

All Glory and Honor forever remains to
the Father, the Son, and the Holy Spirit.

PREFACE

The word Hope is defined as being optimistic, having expectation, having courage. But sometimes life happens in such a way that leaves us with a sense of defeat and without realizing it at first, it permeates our lives. This book was written to change that. We all need to hear or read a positive word on a regular basis because it feeds into our lives and in turn, in the lives around us. I have sought to make the purpose of this book to be a source of encouragement to the person who has faced a struggle or two and, in the end, lost the battle which can make you wonder why even try? This is where my message comes in. There is HOPE beyond all that. Hope that has your future marked with a fresh understanding of who you are and not who you were, and where you are going and not where you have been. *Hope* can lead you *Beyond* all that.

In this book, I have included the experiences of people that I personally know whose lives were affected by the power that hope can give. Each person faced real life heartache, real life disappointments and real-life failures that had defeat written all over their experience. But Truth had a message for each one and it was based on Hope. Please let each message speak to you and provide encouragement to your heart and be the balm that brings hope and renewal to any area of defeat you have faced. Let me add that this is not an attempt to convince you of my point of view. This book was written to provide you with information based on truth that has proven to be effective in their lives and countless more besides. Truth has its own power, and I believe you will see it in reality as you read through each story.

I believe you would agree that it is amazing how the human spirit can endure great tragedy and heartache, but somehow still manage to bounce back. But we also understand that every person has their own level of tolerance in dealing with the harsh circumstances of life. Sometimes we do *not* bounce back so easily, and we wonder how we can regain our footing. Sometimes, we wonder *if* we will.

That is where hope comes in. I know that if you are having a difficult time getting beyond a very challenging circumstance of life, hope can and will make a difference if you grab hold of it and do not let go. Please read on to see for yourself the life-affirming power of Hope. God's purpose can still prevail in your life - IF you choose to trust Him. Don't limit Him by your circumstances, past or present. He is much greater than that!

Myra Woodbridge

"And now, Lord, what do I wait for? My hope is in You."

Psalm 39: 7

CONTENTS

Chapter One

For The Record

All good parents begin teaching their kids the basics from an early age and work their way through their development. I can still see in my mind's eye the day my dad and my brother taught me how to ride a bike! What a comedy that would have been for all to see. For the record: I caught on to how to pedal the bike well. It just happened to be in the wrong direction! I had a fleeting sense of defeat that afternoon! My brother was a little less patient with me than dad, but I finally got the idea! If only all learning experiences were so easy to regroup from and start moving in the right direction.

Life became a lot more complicated than learning to ride a bike of course. My parents sought to teach all three of their children to make the best decisions they could so we could avoid as many catastrophes as possible and the mean sense of defeat that comes with them. But life comes knocking and catastrophes are unavoidable, so you learn to deal with them. The aspect of defeat adds a flavor to catastrophes that you never enjoy.

There was one thing my dad told me that I still remember.

I would not be surprised if your parents told you the *same thing* and have been taught by you to your own children. Here it is: "You can do anything that you set your mind to do." Am I right? You *have* heard that from your own parents? AND taught by you in your family unit? Yes. For the Record…I agree with my father. He was right about this and about many other things, as was my mother! (I can imagine both of them reading this from their view from heaven and smiling at each other that I finally agreed with them on something! Teen age girls aren't known for being real agreeable with their parents about very much at all. But – for the record – I will go ahead and admit that my mother and dad were right about a <u>lot</u> of things…but this is just between us.)

There is something more I have learned about the guidance my dad gave me. It is this: there must be parameters to doing anything you set your mind to do. The "anything" you want to do must be the right direction for *you* to do. You might say, well sure. But sometimes we are subject to jump in head first and not think it through in the way it deserves.

Just think in these terms for a moment… If you are a Christian, any direction you take must have God's seal of approval on it. In other words, it can't be anything that would lead us in a direction that is not God's plan or purpose for our lives. If you find yourselves in that position, please consider changing direction as soon as possible because the wrong direction for the right reason will still lead you wrong. It may take you longer to reach your goal by choosing the right direction but the wrong direction will take you places that will only add sorrow upon sorrow to your life and defeat will be inevitable. I can give you an example of this. It is a pretty simple one but it makes my point.

This experience happened in my earlier years of serving the Lord. I was asked to play the piano for someone who was starting out in evangelistic ministry. (I'm sure my being asked was more out of convenience for them, than my being real gifted in playing...I'm not trying to be humble, I'm just a realist.)

When I was asked to do this, I knew in my heart that would not be anything I could do for several reasons. The most important one was....I knew that was not for me on any level. It was not my calling. I mention this to show you how we can get drawn into something that is "good" and is for a good reason but if I agreed to do something that the Lord did not direct me to explicitly do, then I would have been following a person's lead and not the Lord's.

If we jump ahead of the Lord's purpose for our lives, it is a leap into unnecessary errors that can complicate life for us, including opening the door to possible defeat in some way. I'm not into complications under any circumstances! It is our responsibility to follow the Lord's lead and not another person and not ourselves. Even with following the path the Lord has for us to walk, there are going to be challenges without adding to them of our own making.

The best safeguard is to pray and wait on the Lord for His leadership in our lives. He does not act on impulse or by our time clock to communicate His will to us. How much better it would be if we used our waiting time to get to know Him and, in our fellowship together, He reveals His will in our decision making. It is a win-win situation!

We also understand that difficulties *while in God's will* can happen when you least expect it. Jesus warned His disciples about this in John 16: 33 where He said "These things I have spoken to you, that in Me you may have peace. In the world you will have tribulation; but be of good cheer, I have overcome the world."

This statement by Christ makes it clear that adversity is not just a very real possibility – it is inevitable as a consequence of living on planet earth. The word 'tribulation' is the real indicator here! It alerts you that something very uncomfortable and unwanted is subject to happen. The word means pressure, anguish, squashing, adversity. You can relate it to the crushing of grapes or olives in a press. That is harsh treatment! That is extreme pressure and that can be life in this world at times. I'm sure none of us are fans of adversity! But on the flip side, the Lord has promised His grace and strength because He knows our weaknesses! We are not self-sufficient and we should never pretend to be so! He will enable us to endure and not surrender to the negatives around us or allow them within our own spirit.

That might be one of the worst defeats that can happen to someone!

Defeat can happen to the best of people, the handsome, the beautiful, the smart, the successful. It comes in all sizes, colors and distinctions. It can be a failed marriage you never envisioned could happen, leaving you to be a broken family with broken hearts, or perhaps it is a betrayal by someone you held in high esteem, or it might be a rebellious child, a relationship that you just knew would last but soured without warning, a business that you devoted yourself to but could not make it work, a long season of health issues, abuse by someone who should have your best interests at heart and protect you but did not, they did not value you as you deserve. The list could go on Ad Infinitum. There are so many ways defeat can rear its ugly head.

I can't imagine anyone who has not had some measure of defeat in their lives, all worthy of compassion and understanding. But these circumstances are not lost to the redeeming power of God! It is possible to come back from any defeat and learn from our experience and then take that knowledge into our future and be able to help someone else.

There is a beautiful passage in the first epistle written by Peter in chapter 1: 6-7. His letter was not to believers who were living it up on the Rivera without a care in the world. No. He wrote to Christians who were suffering for their faith due to intense persecution. He did not tell them that all their suffering would be over soon and all would be well for them from then on. He had something better to tell them than that! Here are his words: "In this you greatly rejoice, though now for a little while, if need be, you have been grieved by various trials, that the genuineness of your <u>faith</u>, being <u>much more precious than gold</u> that perishes, though it is tested by fire, may be found to praise, honor, and glory at the revelation of Jesus Christ."

Such a profound outlook about a person's faith in Christ! He declared to them it "was much <u>more</u> precious than gold."! Gold is the same then as it is now. It is expensive. Very expensive. It is a precious commodity. According to Wikipedia, in most mining operations, every ton of ore only produces <10 grams of gold! That means 1 ton = .0005% gold and that only 2500 tons are mined in a year. That is a lot of hard work, expertise, knowledge of equipment and the mine itself and willpower. To be sure – nothing of value happens without determination and an understanding of worth. As expensive as this tally would be in order to mine the gold and as much value as people place on gold, it doesn't hold a candle to a person who has faith in the Lord. Anything can happen to earthly gold as with anything else on this planet. But a person's faith in God supersedes in comparison and is of much greater value!

Of all the words that Peter could have used to describe faith, he used "precious". In the Greek language of the New Testament, it simply means costly. It is such because of the high price the Lord Jesus paid for us to have it birthed in our hearts! Faith in God, in His Son, in the Holy Spirit and in His Word is how we live on this earth. Hebrews 11: 6 tells us "But without faith it is impossible to please Him, for he who comes to God must believe that He is, and He is a rewarder of those who diligently seek Him." Our faith rest in the finished work of Christ or it rests in nothing at all. And for the record - It is that valuable.

"Let your mercy, O Lord, be upon us, just as we hope in You."

Psalm 33: 22

Chapter Two

Stuck On Page 99

We have all been there when we are reading a book, a magazine, or a newspaper or whatever, but we are not *really* reading the words...we are a million miles away, our mind on whatever is troubling us. We are stuck on the same page, on the same sentence. It is immaterial what the reading material is about! Our *thoughts* hinder our reading. They hinder our life, in fact!

That is how defeat can affect us. It swoops in and refuses to let go unless or until we can get it resolved in our mind. I want to provide ways that can help you do that because I know what it feels like. I had to learn how to *turn the page* on defeat! I'm sure you could say the same thing! Please keep in mind that God doesn't *cause* our defeats. They come in the package of Life itself. God wants to be there for us, to strengthen us through our adversity and bless us to *overcome* the stumbling block of defeat.

In the pages ahead, I will be sharing a few testimonies of some who have done this very thing. They are people who – in the midst of their own struggles with defeat – found their answer – it was Hope birthed out of faith in God that enabled them to see their circumstance in a different light!

The first person I want to introduce you to was someone we never knew until she arrived at our front door late one Saturday night, more than ten years ago. It was a memorable evening! Terry and I were getting an early start for bed because we 'rise and shine' on Sunday mornings due to our scheduled teaching of an adult class at church. It just so happened that at this very point in time, Terry and I were discussing some of the Scripture that would be covered in class. *This is an important fact in our story.* As we are sitting there in our living room, we hear a knock at our front door! Needless to say - it shocked us! We live out in the country, in a very quiet neighborhood, so we took our time answering, giving ourselves time to see if we recognized the person at the door. We did not. There was a light rain falling at the time, as well. Who would be out in the rain, coming to someone's home that you did not know? Well, your mind races with all kinds of answers and none of them were particularly encouraging!

When Terry opened the door, there stood a middle aged woman, a little disheveled, whom we did not know. She soon introduced herself, but I will only give her name by an initial, Mrs. S. We had never seen her before! It was obvious that she was very upset, very emotional and we were on tap to do something for her! But what?? Was her car broken down? Was she lost? Was she abandoned? It was perplexing to us but we had to wait it out to hear her story. What would cause someone to be out and about at night and come to someone's home she did not know? Physically she was not an imposing person that would cause you to be afraid but still…. (I admit that I do like good mystery movies but when the mystery comes to your own front door….Not so much.) Terry didn't seem afraid one bit so I decided he was the better judge of the situation than I so I started to relax.

I will admit that we did look around outside the front door – casually - just to make sure there wasn't anyone else standing on the other side of her, just waiting to rush in. We could not detect anyone else. We asked her inside and she began to tell us her story. She explained that she was the neighbor who lived on the street behind us. She was desperate. Not a good sign. She spoke freely but was obviously distraught.

We sought to calm her and "kinda, sorta" did. Really, we were not absolutely sure how to approach the situation. We were simply winging it. The lady was part upset and part afraid. We continued to feel our way through the experience. We didn't want to rush her so we sought to be patient in giving her time to explain what her problem was.

As it turned out she and her husband – both in their 60's, I believe – had an adult son in their home. The son and father were having an argument and it was so upsetting that she had to flee! We understood that but we were quietly in disbelief as to *how* she maneuvered through the woods and brush that are between the two houses! That should have taken a few minutes to do, considering it was dark and lightly raining. She could have injured herself badly as well. But she was determined to get away. And she made it to our doorstep safely. Perhaps there were angels walking with her. I would have wanted a host of them if I had attempted to do the same thing as she did! (I am not a risk taker on any level!)

As we listened to her, neither Terry nor I doubted any longer that the Lord had directed her to our doorstep. She conveyed her story to us that as she came closer to the house, she stopped at the front bay window – keep in mind that it is very quiet at night where we live, and this little lady stopped to *listen* to our voices! Remember what we were talking about prior to her coming? Yes, the Scripture. When she heard *that,* she then had peace to knock on our door for help and safety. The Lord was with all of us! We listened to her as she shared her despair and concerns for the ones she loved so dearly. We continued to be listening ears and extended consolation to her. We talked to her about the Lord and possible solutions, seeking to give her a new sense of strength but also hope that He could change things in their home, and we prayed together. When she felt comfortable to go home, she called her husband and he came to pick her up, which he did. I'm sure they had an interesting discussion as they drove back. Or a quiet one! I don't know, of course.

When she was about to leave, we stood up to walk her to the door. That is when Terry asked her if she likes to read. I thought, "why are you asking her that"?? Well, no sooner than he asked, she answered yes. That is when Terry asked me to get a copy of the first book I ever wrote "Chosen of the Lord, Broken in Heart" to give to her. I wasn't sure about doing that because I wasn't sure if she was just being nice in accepting it or if she really was interested. But since Terry asked me to do that, I went ahead and got her the book. I signed it and gave it to her. We welcomed her to come to our home anytime. And with that, she made her way out to ride home with her husband. (I can't imagine their conversation as they drove!) It was perfectly clear at that point, that she felt such despair that she would seek refuge outside of her own home. We were thankful that the Lord chose our home as that refuge. We trusted that things had settled down there and everyone could pursue peace among themselves again.

As it turned out, that was not the last time we would see her. It was only a matter of a few weeks after that experience that this little lady paid us a second surprise visit. This time, it was for a different reason. She wanted us to know the sad news that her husband passed away due to health issues that had not been dealt with. She wanted to tell me how much my book meant to her because she had really struggled with questions relating to her faith and if she had failed him as his wife and caretaker. Did she fail to pray enough? She would ask the Lord why it had to happen? Could she have done more? Did she fail to recognize how sick he really was? She had so many "whys" and "what ifs" troubling her mind and heart. Her pain sought to blame someone, even if it was herself. The Lord already had the answer for her. She needed peace. She needed hope again for *her* life.

After his passing, her mind was filled with a lot of "whys and what ifs?" concerning it. She was so troubled with thoughts that she failed to do enough for him, that if she had done this or that, he may still be alive. She questioned the Lord as to why it had to happen and on and on. She felt guilty as if she failed him! Her pain sought to blame someone, even if it was herself. She had been in terrible turmoil, but the Lord already had the answer for her.

Mrs. S. was a person of faith, but her circumstance was making it difficult to reconcile her faith and her life experience that caused so much anguish for her and understandably so. But she read my book, from start to finish in one night, and the Lord used our testimony to help *restore her peace again* and helped her see that self-blame, with the nagging sense of defeat, was not the answer. It would change *nothing*! The peace that God gave her helped her to understand that there are things in this life that happen that we cannot control, nor dictate. There are so many things about life and living that are not up for debate with the Lord. He alone is sovereign and has the wisdom to make the best choice in any of life's circumstances. He will strengthen us to get from point A to point B and beyond safely when it is so hard for us to navigate the journey of life with its twists and turns. She had a renewed sense of hope again. She was at peace with the understanding that the Lord controls the times and the seasons for every purpose under heaven and not mere people (Ecclesiastes 3:1). She would live each day with the Lord's help. Before she left, she told us she wanted to buy copies of my book for her family and friends! We didn't mind that at all. Fortunately, I had enough for her to take with her.

The entire experience was a tremendous blessing for us to see how the Lord orchestrates events and people and timing, for that one individual who needed someone to show care and concern and prayer. It was very rewarding that God chose to use my personal experience of feeling defeated, how it affected my health, how the Lord brought me through that, and how it came to be the very testimony that she needed to read! It helped her continue with the next step in the new season of her life.

We have to think about the goodness of God in this – how Terry and I just happened to be talking about the Scripture just at the time that this lady – *unseen by us as it was happening* but known by God - was in search of a safe haven, and that was the very thing that gave her assurance that our home was the place to visit. Only the Lord can orchestrate connections like this and you never see it coming! Nothing is happenstance in the lives that belong to Him. I'm thankful that He is in control.

My point in telling you this, is however severe your defeat is, the Lord enable you – even if it seems gradual – to rise above it, step it and move on in peace and have hope restored to your heart and the consequence to others will be that *your* experience becomes a testimony that can lift their load of despair so that their journey is lighter too. Yes, we *can* look up to the Lord in prayer and move on and not look back – We can finally - *Turn The Page*!

> *"My voice You shall hear in the morning, O Lord; In the morning I will direct my prayer to You, and I will look up."*
>
> *Psalm 5: 3*

Chapter Three

Hope Shines Through!

O ur next testimony goes back to someone I met in 1973 by the name of Pat Heiselman (name is used by permission.) We met purely by "accident on purpose"! It was a meeting that the Lord arranged for both of us. At that time, I was at the piano in the church sanctuary practicing for the children's VBS program. It happened on that particular morning that Pat quietly walked in, sat down on the pew in front of me and told me "Myra, the devil is trying to kill me!" I looked at her as though she was speaking in a foreign language because it did not register to me in English. I was not very knowledgeable at that time on how the enemy can set the stage for circumstances that are equally frustrating *and* harmful. I soon learned the reason behind Pat's concern, but it was all resolved. I will go ahead and tell you the enemy's plot was not successful for which we are thankful! She is still with us and continues to serve the Lord!

From that point on, Pat and I developed a lifelong friendship that is still very dear and precious to us both. I could not guess the hours we have spent in conversation and much laughter and many times in prayer together and the Lord was gracious to answer! We do not live in the same state any longer, but we are still each other's confidant and encourager. It is amazing how well we still know one another today! Distance doesn't separate friendships like we have which is such a blessing from the Lord.

Pat did not have a happy home life as a child. She was raised by her single mom and her grandmother. She had cousins, aunts, and uncles but she never knew her real dad. Her mom eventually married a man who was not interested in caring for Pat. He was verbally abusive and downright mean. He could be very vindictive – even to an innocent child! He and Pat's mom had 3 children of their own and eventually the family unit was more like the 5 of them and Pat on the outskirts of it all - on her own. At her first opportunity, she left home, made her own decisions, lived her own way. Her idea of family was not what she left. She knew it just had to be different than that. Her search was on to discover it for herself.

However, Pat's search was geared in the wrong direction for a long time. She eventually met someone, fell in love, and were married. In time, they had two children. As it turned out, the marriage did not work out. There was a divorce. So far, defeat was following her around, seeking to ruin all hope of a better life than she ever knew. Her two children were the two victories she walked away with. She had to take the steps necessary to see that their lives were better than hers! But how? It would take time for her to discover that.

Pat's life would see a change come about but it would not be a straight shot to a cure! As time went on, she met a man, Carl Heiselman who truly loved her. He also had two children from a previous marriage. Pat and Carl eventually married, and the job of blending families began. It was not an easy task! It seldom is! But they were committed to doing everything they could to make it work.

Things rocked along until there was a visit from Carl's brother, Jerry Heiselman. He came at just the right time. He did not come on a whim. He came on purpose which the family would learn about in due time. He did not reveal exactly what that purpose was right away, but that was wisdom. He came to sow seeds of hope in Pat and in Carl. Hope that would take them and their family beyond their individual defeats of the past and bury them so that they did not cloud the future of their blended family. Listen, that is not an easy task to do! We can't gloss over how hurts and mistreatments and disappointments from childhood on can linger for a long time in a person's spirit. It takes patience and care and love to just begin to see a breakthrough come about. That involves more time and more energy. But Jerry was not in a rush. He was there for the duration.

I will tell you that Pat and Carl were always hospitable people. They welcomed people into their home and at their table all through their married life. Terry and I spent many hours of fellowship with them. When Jerry visited, he did not give any indication of when he would return home. Even after a few weeks…he continued to keep his departure plans to himself. Thanksgiving came and went, but Jerry stayed. Christmas came and went and yes, Jerry was still in town, but he eventually rented his own place. Even so, he continued to sow those subtle seeds of hope that the lives of his family could be different than anything they had ever known. Hope that the defeat of their past would only be a memory of what was, not what would be in their future. Jerry knew himself how that could happen because of his own personal experience.

On a very cold blustery winter night at the midnight hour in January, Jerry stayed for the night at Carl's insistence due to the icy weather that had hit the area. But the Lord had another purpose in mind for Jerry's overnight stay. It was about to unfold. The Lord was ready to reap the spiritual harvest of all those seeds Jerry had sown. Everyone was fast asleep except for Pat and Jerry.

As quiet filled the house, Jerry talked at length with Pat about her life and – at just the right moment, he led her to the Lord right there in their living room. She was born again, not by feeling but by the truth that Jerry showed her in the Scripture. As they were talking about the reality of her new birth experience, a large crashing sound came from the rear of the house! Whatever could have happened! No one could imagine what they would see.

Everyone was certainly awake now and rushed to see the cause of such an awful sound! When they were amazed at what they discovered. It was the large tree that stood outside her young son's bedroom! Half of it broke away due to the icy weight that covered it! How amazing it was that the tree that had always leaned toward the house, on that very night FELL AWAY from it and into a drainage ditch, sparing the life of her only son! There was more than one miracle in that home that cold winter's night! All because one man chose to fulfill his purpose and speak hope and faith and life into the lives of those he cared about. Jerry never gave up. Nor did the Lord.

I wanted to include Pat's story in my book because she has always been a person who forgives quickly and thoroughly. She was ill treated by those who knew better but still did so. That is willful meanness and abuse! It wasn't Pat's fault. It was the awfulness in the hearts of those who mistreated her and who never made it right with her. But I must tell you there is a quality that Pat has that is so remarkable to me because I know more of her story than I will share. I never heard Pat speak of herself as a victim and she always has had a willingness to forgive everyone! She could tell the story and turn the spotlight on them all – but her heart has been so changed since that wintry night when she was born again and her son's life spared that she gave up the hatred of those that hurt her so maliciously, and the desire to retaliate, and to wound others as she had been wounded. I hope you can let the depth of this message sink in and touch your heart to respond to your offenders. Life is not about getting even. It is about living free. Free from the trappings of all manner of offenses. Pat is the prime example of someone who is free.

When Hope shined through that night, Faith and Grace shined through as well. Each part has been obvious in her life since trusting in Christ. It is true that much of it was hard until adulthood, but the Lord radically improved it beyond what she ever thought possible!

I've shared this testimony with you because it is important for people to know and understand that any defeat – whether it originates with our bad decisions or it is a result of evil in another person's heart that hope and faith can turn our lives in the best direction possible - to the Lord, to His purpose for our lives, to His peace, joy, and strength! It IS possible to get beyond any defeat. Hope will always show us how. Let it shine! But it is up to us to receive it.

> "I rise before the dawning of the morning, and
> cry for help; I hope in Your word."
>
> Psalm 119: 147

Chapter Four

The Struggle Is Real

I f there is anything that will hinder our future, it is this: to think in terms of what ifs, what might have been, what I should have done, what now. That only leads to exasperation on our part. We cannot control all the circumstances that life can bring our way. God is not affected by circumstances. He can work in spite of people, places or things and all the circumstances that can result from those people, places or things!

On the other hand, we humans can get caught in all this at times. It is our human nature. Our thought life gets tangled up in the weeds of whatever our crisis is. When this happens, we need to turn off the wrong thoughts and allow faith to lift us up above all that and to deny the circumstance control over our thoughts. This is a lot easier said than done! I know! But it is so worthwhile. This means we need a mental clean up! It is called having our mind renewed. Paul wrote about this in Romans 12:2 "And do not be conformed to this world, but be transformed by the renewing of our mind, that you may prove what is that good and acceptable and perfect will of God." But how do I do this?

Renewing our mind is not complicated. I want to give attention to some key words in this verse above. The word "conformed" simply means to conform to the same pattern of others. In this instance, the Word is directing us to not conform to the patterns of this world's system. This type of system is anti-God, anti-Scripture, anti-Christianity. It is dominated by self-important, self-indulgent supposedly, high-minded people. Conformity to any dogma that is domineering of another person's own ability to make decisions for yourself is totally wrong. If you do not see things their way – then you are written off. I would consider that a blessing! The Lord does not dominate people. He loves people and wants the best for us which is why He sent His Son to die for us.

Also, the next word to point out is "transformed". This has a powerful meaning to it. It is "to care afterwards" which speaks to having done something we regret and then changing our mind or purpose after! That is the power of transformation in our thinking.

Well, regretting an action or word is the starting point to mental clean up. It's the awful moment when you realize you have made a monumental mistake and it requires action on our part to make things right. This is caring about it *after it happened*. How powerful it would be if we could care enough to correct our thinking before doing something regretful. The Lord can help us!

He recently helped me and he used some of *my own words* that I wrote in my last book "The Path Forward"! You could say I was receiving a dose of my own medicine! But that is fine as long as it is good medicine and truth always is. My particular dose that day included not retaliating against someone who hurts my feelings. I was contemplating making a statement that would let someone know how their actions affected me. I didn't have a problem standing up for myself but the *how* of it was the issue. It amounted to being retaliatory. The Lord changed my thinking before I goofed up again! I really do appreciate Him for intercepting my plans and redirecting them in a more positive way. My mind was changed. It was *renewed* in thinking the way the Lord saw things in that matter.

The mind is the seat of emotions and affections. It can get pretty crowded with a lot of negative junk, if we aren't careful. If I allow God's Word to correct my thinking, then my perspective will become clearer and my attitude more positive which leads to a more peaceful life. It starts with asking the Lord to help us in this area, to work on our wrong attitudes that result in wrong behavior. Everyone needs help in this because wrong attitudes will mean we will "care afterwards" when it is too late to change the consequences! Avoiding this is a lot easier than living with regrets because – as you may have experienced – regrets is the road that leads to defeats. They will mount up to block our way if we do not address them. Hope is waiting for us to *choose* to accept personal responsibility to make necessary changes which paves the way for us to get beyond it all.

I sometimes call negative thinking - stinkin' thinkin' because of its power to ruin so much in a person's life. It is the trap of worry and fear. I would suspect that every person alive has at some point worried or fretted or became fearful over something or someone. You don't have to raise your hand. I know you are out there! We all are in the same boat! It is called being human. We see with our eyes how bad things look or we hear the awful reports day in, day out on the news or social media. Worry can start. Fear seeks to take hold! But none of that affects the circumstance! It is understandable. It just isn't helpful on any level!

The problem only gets worse because worry and fear will only lead to more worry, more fretting and more frustration. Eventually – sooner rather than later – fear seeks to take up residence. We cannot allow that to happen. It will take up residence in our minds if we do not get a handle on it! It is a thief and a robber! It robs us of peace, joy, and contentment. Our answer is to follow the instruction of Scripture.

The apostle Peter could tell you that he knows what I am talking about because he had his issues of seeing how bad things looked and letting how his perception of the circumstances lead him to make some really bad choices, and he experienced a personal failure! He had to overcome the fact that when Jesus needed him the most, he denied Him three times. He carried the weight of defeat on his heart and mind until after the resurrection when Jesus sought him out to re-claim him to his purpose in the Kingdom of God! Jesus did not condemn him. He rescued him and Peter made things right with the Lord and he moved on to live out the rest of his life serving the Lord with a faithful heart, winning thousands to the Lord with his first sermon! His experience testifies to us still today and his writing in his first epistle carries the significance of this testimony.

Defeat is not an attitude to embrace. It is a weapon meant to tear you down and keep you from rising again. It comes in to take over and rule our lives. It doesn't dance around and appear harmless. It comes in to tell you flat footed what a horrible mistake you made and how you will never recover from it. It likes to hang around, hang on and rear its ugly head to remind us at every opportunity. The result is it can become a mindset that lurks around in our thoughts to convince us of "why bother trying"; "you failed before"; "no one is interested".… "you will never have another opportunity". This oppressive mindset originates from the coffers of satan, even if it was a person who spoke it to you or over you at some point in your life. That person is used of the enemy.

People can function in this type of accusatory behavior to make others as miserable as they are! But I want to assure you of this truth: regardless of how wrong we may be in any given matter; God does not write us off. He does not accuse us of anything. He will correct us when we are wrong, but He doesn't accuse. He has our best interests at heart and wants to rescue us in our times of defeat. Satan is called the accuser of the brethren in Scripture (Revelations 12: 10) because that is his nature. The word carries the meaning of condemning someone. Without hope, no less.

This is how our enemy works. He seizes any opportunity he can to use his ammunition of accusations and clothes them in thoughts to our mind to debilitate us and bring our future to a standstill and render our faith and our hope ineffective! We cannot let him succeed in this and the Lord will direct us how.

It starts with us asking the Lord for His help in changing our defeated mindset! The consequence of not changing our thinking, of not allowing our mind to be renewed, will be that our lives will remain snagged on that one occasion, or that one failure or series of failures, that awful regret of oneself or someone else, or that terrible mistreatment that was totally unjustified and malicious. It isn't worth it! This type of mindset describes thinking that is unprofitable and unproductive on every level! It turns our thoughts inward, not upward in faith toward God and His promises and not forward in the direction God has intended for us. (Remember, God leads us forward not backward unless it is to correct a wrongdoing.) This mindset magnifies our mistakes and translates them into defeat! These thoughts rob us of our peace and our joy in life. This is not a part of God's plan for us at all. Let's determine to trust in *His* plan and not the plan of defeat.

"Let the words of my mouth and the meditation of my heart be acceptable in Your sight, O Lord, my strength and my Redeemer."

Psalm 19: 14

Chapter Five

Hope Greater Than Our Weaknesses

I have an additional testimony to share with you. It is the testimony of a dear friend of ours that reflects the grace of God and His great mercy. Because of both, Hope was renewed in his life at just the right time.

I met James several years ago. He was a business associate of Terry's. Both are retired now but they continue to keep in touch. I wanted to include him in my book because his experience teaches us about Hope on another level – a very important level it is.

James grew up with parents that loved him and gave him the benefit of Christian influence at home and in a loving church setting. When he was still a pre-teen, he same to learn of his parent's marriage problems. It became obvious that the problems went deep and they divorced. This was a crushing blow when his mom told him of their plans. He loved his dad and mom and wanted his family to be whole again. He prayed earnestly for that to happen. However, the breach was too great and a young boy's prayers went unanswered. He was devastated and that followed him through his teen years, causing him to reject his faith and he began down a path totally opposite of his upbringing. He began experimenting with drugs and alcohol. The enemy of James' soul caused this setup in his family to not only break up his parent's marriage but to also take down James as well. It would be a dark path that James began to travel.

He eventually attended college as a young man, but his main focus was on his lifestyle of drugs and alcohol. He eventually married only to have that fail. His wife could not handle his divided heart of loving the drugs and alcohol more than he loved her. He would seek pastoral counsel, as well as AA and he would do well for a season only to fail and give up again. But God's grace refused to give up on James.

There have been many people that God has used through the years of his rebellion to reach out to James and seek to influence him to have Hope again; to trust again in God's goodness and love for him and to get the help he needed to get drugs and alcohol out of his life once and for all. It was a struggle. A very real struggle. He might be sober for 2 or 3 years only to relapse and fall into the same pattern of drugs and alcohol and moral failures. Would his life ever be whole again? Could Hope ever be in his heart again? It could and it did.

He married a lovely lady in 2000 who was a Christian, and things started shaping up in his life. The glimmer of Hope seemed to shine a bit more for James after all. In 2022 that glimmer was practically snuffed out when James fell off the wagon again while alone at home, drinking from his hidden stash of vodka when his wife was out of town. This sounds pretty forlorn for James, but there is something about Hope that is derived from the reality of God's goodness and mercy and never-ending love that would disagree. Just when you think it is all over for you – God shines on your life and Hope is renewed once again in your heart! Oddly enough it happened that night as he was all alone drinking himself to the bottom of the bottle.

An onlooker might think this experience spelled complete defeat for James, but I can tell you that it wasn't the end. It was the beginning of clarity to his heart that he had finally reached bottom BUT it was not the end of him! Hope made sure of this. God zeroed in on James' personal issues – just between him and God. Before, he could always justify his sin in "some warped way" as he described to me. Not this time. God wouldn't let him do that again. It was decision time. It was his time to be set free from that which plagued him and had nearly ruined his entire life. Sin doesn't just happen in a fleeting moment. It comes in to dominate and take control. Only God's greater power can redeem that and transform a person's life and restore Hope so that even though he had experienced failure after failure, he could leave it all at the foot of the cross and know that with his heart changed, his life would be changed as well. A life of joy and contentment in Christ was now his.

I want to emphasize this truth. Yes, James was a broken soul for a lot of years. His life was in shambles a good part of the time! Yet, God knew where James was at all times. He wasn't pleased that James was living as he was, but His grace would not let go. He would still draw James' heart to trust in Him and to live for Him again. It was an up and down cycle that Grace had to ride with him so that when he finally reached bottom, Grace was right there to scoop him up and get him back on track with the Lord in a firm and solid way. Hope did not desert him. Faith may have been low, but it was never really out. It just needed refueling! God's love was extended to him over and over again. It finally won! James is living in peace with his wife and is serving the Lord and involved in ministries to help those going through the same struggles he did.

I have shared this testimony for people to understand that even Christian people struggle with different issues just like everyone else. The church is full of people with weaknesses and flaws! We simply have come to understand that we are all in various levels of progress in need of God's strength and grace each day. He loves us enough to be there for us to help us in our weakness so that we can overcome and move on. We must not write people off if they have a pattern of failing, succeeding, only to fail again, succeed again, etc. It means we need to continue to pray for them and extend mercy and hope that their lives can be different. They can be whole again and stay that way by the Grace and Power of God! Redemption takes time in some people's lives when their lives were so fragmented by circumstances they had no control over and other circumstances of which they can't get control within themselves! Think about it! We can be assured that it will be fully accomplished and the person's life made whole when we refuse to give up on them! Just imagine how disappointed the Lord might be if any one of the Christian people that He put in James' life at different times on his journey, had turned their back on him! We are thankful that Grace did not let that happen.

James' story reminds me of a story in Luke's gospel of a woman whose life was fragmented by sin but she heard about Jesus and faith arose in her heart that perhaps He could put the pieces of her life together to be totally different than she ever knew! She learned that He was visiting in the home of a religious leader - and she went there! She was not invited, nor would she have ever been invited! The religious leader recognized her as soon as he saw her. (I wonder how??) She was thought to have been a prostitute. He referred to her as nothing more than a "sinner". One who is not a part of his congregation! How could she ever fit in? Never! at least by his standards. But it wasn't his standards that caused her to make her way into his home.

I believe her faith and her hope for a changed life spurred her on to the point she did not concern herself with it pleasing anyone if she walked right in and made her way to Jesus. Because that is exactly what she did. You can read about it in Luke 7: 36-50. This woman was so moved by being in the Lord's presence that she stood at his feet weeping. She wept to such a degree that she could wash His feet with those tears and then dried them with her hair. She then kissed His feet and anointed them with the fragrant oil that she brought with her.

The entire scene was very disturbing to the religious leader. He was appalled, one might say. The Lord had a word of correction for him. He spoke to him of two debtors, one owing a substantial amount and the other one a small amount. The creditor determined to forgive both debts. Jesus asked the leader which one of the debtors would love his creditor more? The leader had to say the only answer possible. The one that was forgiven much. For once, in the entire story, the religious leader was able to get something right!

The Lord went on to tell him the reasons why he was right. The woman came in and from that moment she only focused on ministering to him, to washing His feet with her own tears and drying them with her hair and kissing His feet. It was customary for anyone who had a guest in their home to see to it that their feet were washed after traveling through the sandy soil to get there. It was a courtesy! Jesus went on to tell the man of how he never greeted Him with a kiss as was also customary, nor did he anoint His head (which was the easier thing to do) as the woman did His feet. It seems the religious leader only did what he had to do for Jesus. He missed the only opportunity he had to do so. How sad!

Her actions proved her profound love for Jesus and caused Jesus to verbally forgive her sins which were many, as he declared to her personally. And He welcomed her to Himself, which the religious leader could not bring himself to do!

When you consider the actions of the three in this story, there was one Giver (Christ), one receiver (the woman) and one faultfinder (the religious leader). I know the One I want to follow and the one I admire for her sacrifice and willingness to risk the ridicule of the man's home in which she entered. I also know the one I never want to be like who was judgmental and critical.

May all our eyes be open to recognize how we all need to care more about helping people find their way out of the messes they get in instead of casting them aside to suffer alone. We aren't called to be fault finders. We are called to be soul winners.

I thank God for all those who encouraged James through the years – Terry being one of them – who refused to give up on a man who needed a breakthrough and received it in a place called Rock Bottom. If you are there or know someone else who is, reach out to the Lord and let Him touch your life to once again bring Hope to your heart for a better life that has a better outcome!

> *"The Path of the just is like the shining sun, that shines ever brighter unto the perfect day."*
>
> *Proverbs 4: 18*

Chapter Six

Hope Can Give Us A Turnaround

The next person I want to tell you about is a man who faced a very frightening situation that proved too big for him to handle. It brought a lot of fear into his mind, and it dominated his actions that led him to make some shocking choices! It might surprise you because he was a successful man, a highly respected person who lived a life of integrity. He always seemed to have the right answer for every situation. There wasn't anything that seemed to trip him up. Until something did. Or rather, someone – a woman who posed a great threat to him!

The man I am writing about is someone straight out of the Bible. You might ask, what does the experience of an Old Testament prophet offer to me in the 21st century?? I would tell you quite a lot actually. I want you to give me the opportunity to tell you a true story about a prophet named Elijah because his experience can tell us a lot about defeat and rising from it. I think if you will read on of his story here that you will see the reality that life happens to everyone, in every generation, whether you are a believer in God or not. His life experience serves us all very well because the truth that it reveals can speak to all who will be open to hearing it! Keep in mind, life is temporary, truth is eternal so truth will always be truth and can speak to us and teach us regardless of the century in which we live.

His experience serves to prove my point that anyone can lose their perspective as it did him, when faced with an overwhelming situation that challenged him as he had never been before. Yes, he lived a devoted life to the Lord and to his ministry, but after all, he was still a human being that was subject to having a wrong perspective about things that led to an error in judgment! When this happened, he went in a totally different direction that was not God's will for him. He would discover that he had to change his *thinking* if he was ever going to go forward in life. Have you ever had to change your mind in order to move forward? Perhaps you have more in common with this man than you think.

You might wonder if Elijah was very young in the Lord and lacked the maturity to handle the situation. No, that wasn't the case. The debacle happened after he had been serving the Lord for a very long time! Defeat does not have a time stamp on it nor an identity stamp. So, it is best to accept our humanity that it is possible to fail but also accept the fact that Hope can always help us recover and even give us a turnaround!

It is true that prophets were an essential part of the spiritual fabric of Israel. They brought the word of the Lord verbally to the people, and they relied upon the prophets to give them direction when facing difficulties. Their instructions would mean life or death to Isreal, depending on their own willingness to follow God's word for them.

The story I want to focus on is found in the Old Testament in I Kings 18. The occasion here concerns the consequences of Elijah's magnificent defeat of the false prophets in the previous chapter. God manifested His awesome power before the eyes of all the people – especially the false prophets. This was an amazing intervention by the Lord in the life and ministry of his servant, Elijah. Yet, in I Kings 19 we do not see the conquering hero, Elijah. We see the despondent soul of Elijah.

Elijah's sadness is caused by the threat of one woman, Jezebel. Elijah had all 450 of her prophets executed because they led Israel away from the true God of their fathers. Jezebel was married to Ahab who was king of Isreal for 22 years. (A point of interest: there really was a woman named Jezebel. She functioned in a seducing, manipulative spirit. If you have ever heard someone called that, now you know why. It is not a compliment!) This marriage was not a match made in heaven. Jezebel came into the relationship as an idol worshipper. It wasn't long at all that Ahab turned to his wife's god and worshipped him. It matters who we marry!

When Jezebel learned of Elijah's victory over the prophets of her god, Baal, she vowed to execute him. She sent a message to him to this effect. She could not dispute that her god was actually the false god whom the prophets served. She only wanted to destroy the person who revealed that fact in front of Israel! One thing that is always obvious – a liar does not respect truth and will try to destroy it. It happens quite often in our world.

When Elijah received this message from Jezebel, he did not send word back that he would like to talk things out with her and see if there could be a compromise. He knew that someone so consumed with hatred and disregard for the one true God, would not be interested in a one-on-one conversation with him. This was not a matter for discussion between reasonable adults. It was a matter of the true God vs a false god. Keep in mind, the false one: is dead. Yes, all false religions have this in common. They have nothing to offer mankind that is life-affirming. Their purpose is to misguide people until they fall into the same ditch they are in.

If you read I Kings 19: 3, you will read Elijah's prompt response to Jezebel. He dropped everything – including the written threat – and ran for his life – not just a few miles down the road. No, he ran for 200 miles down the road into southern Judah! When he arrived there, he didn't linger. He left his servant at that location and took off on another day's journey into the wilderness! I believe we can all agree that this successful prophet was now in a defeated mindset.

Verse 4 of chapter 19 tells us that he left the area of his greatest victory and went to the southernmost part of Judah.... far away from that Jezebel. Let me just say, Elijah didn't just *leave* the area. He ran from it! What moved this mighty man of power! His emotions! There are positive, wonderful emotions in our hearts but there are some real losers too. If we allow our emotions to control us, we will live defeated lives until we decide to live differently. Any emotion (ours or someone else's) that manipulates us into an action that is counter-productive is not a positive emotion; it is one that needs to be brought under control! Fear is a huge negative emotion. It led Elijah to go away from his purpose and run and hide from Jezebel.

He was frightened of this woman and her wicked plans! He knew she was evil enough to carry out her vow against him. So, he thought it all out in about 2 seconds and his conclusion was to run. His own fearful mind perceived the threat was too real to ignore! He had to take action! He had to find the solution! He had to get beyond defeat his own way!

No one can throw any stones at Elijah for being human enough to let fear of a mean, wicked woman make him run! We can be just as weak in our own way when we are confronted with situations that spell personal DEFEAT! We want to pack up and move out, move on. But, God did not destine us to run when something goes wrong, even if the threat is real or we totally miss the mark and the entire situation is our fault. God wants us to stand flat footed and face the music, stand the test, and dare to trust in Him to get us through it all.

I believe the Lord wants us to view our circumstance – however it is defined, or from wherever it originates, through the eyes of HOPE. Don't roll your eyes! This is something we must discipline ourselves to do! It can start today. You can begin today to make a quality decision that "with God's help, I want to view any circumstance of life that comes my way through the prism of Hope and Faith, that God is infinitely greater than all that I am experiencing in this present moment!

This is possible when our FAITH rises up within us and we determine to believe God's promises to us, then HOPE strengthens us to expect God's help in the matter! Yes, we make mistakes. Yes, we may be discouraged about it all. But Hope would tell us: don't stay in the isolated place of *dwelling mentally* on how bad things look or how awful our mistake was! To do so only hinders our lives even more! It is time to make a change! But how do we do that?

It all goes back to changing our mindset as I wrote of earlier. If we ever give in to the negative thoughts and allow them to trouble our mind day in, day out, we will never see all that God has planned for us. This is a tactical move we must make with the Lord's help. It is a move that Elijah finally made. It was the first positive move he made after receiving that threatening message from Jezebel! Listen – the Jezebel that troubled Elijah is physically dead but the one she served still tries to steal, kill and destroy every single day. (John 10: 10). We are not at a loss to overcome these attempts to derail our lives. God's Word gives us the means to do so in Ephesians 6: 10-18 which is a lesson for another day/book!

Elijah's story continues in I Kings 19 when he was at a loss to see beyond the little tree he was sleeping under. His prayer reflected that! He was convinced that his only answer was to just give up and die. (I guess he forgot that Jezebel would have accommodated him on that wish but….he still prayed that way.) How was he convinced that he had nothing to live for anymore??? *His thoughts told him so*! His specific thoughts of *defeat* were in control!

While hiding out in a wilderness, Elijah prayed this sorrowful prayer, telling the Lord to just take his life. *He wanted to escape*! He might as well have prayed: "Take me out of this mess so I can be free from Jezebel's grasp!" He didn't pray that but he was just as pitiful. He had no answers for his predicament. But God did, he just never asked the Lord for HIS take on things!

After this sorrowful prayer, Elijah went to sleep. What else was there for him to do! He was a failure! He was defeated! *But not in reality*! Again, it was only in *his thought life* that he was defeated! He had tremendous success until the moment he read the message from Jezebel!! Just one threat from a sinister, evil woman caused Elijah to *rethink himself*. This is a critical point for us to consider! Our lives can get turned upside down the moment we allow <u>any</u> <u>person to cause us to rethink ourselves</u>. As a result, defeat had crept into his thinking. He *thought* defeat and he *acted* defeated. Running away from our circumstances indicates how defeated we see ourselves and our life.

The only One in this story that was <u>not</u> defeated was the Lord, Himself! He wasn't in agreement with Elijah's perspective.

He had a plan all in place! He would have to get the attention of His prophet to make it known to him. Be assured that God understands our disappointments, our heartaches, our fears and our frustrations in life. He just doesn't want us to *live* sad or dejected, fearful…or defeated. If we will trust Him and in the plan He gives us, letting Hope arise in our hearts, we will get beyond it all. Elijah eventually did so as we will soon see.

In the next few verses, Elijah's story continues on how an angel supplied food for him for the next leg of his journey instead of staying where he was which was under an insignificant tree. His location was known by God wherever he was. The Lord is always several steps ahead of us and His plan for Elijah had not changed! God's provision of food for him by an angel was not to simply fill his stomach at that moment, but for his JOURNEY to return to God's purpose for his life!

After Elijah was physically strengthened by rest and food, Elijah left there and headed for Horeb, the mountain top of God, as it is called. He finds himself a cave in that mountain in which to stay. God must have been waiting on him to get there because right away, He asks Elijah: "What are you doing here, Elijah?" Elijah began to tell the Lord how spiritual he was… talking about how zealous he was for the Lord. That it was His people Israel who were the ones who had forsaken His covenant and torn down His altars and killed His prophets with the sword. Then he told the Lord, "I am the only one you have left, and they seek my life too!" Elijah spread the blame around for everyone but himself. We do the same thing, don't we!

Elijiah was so wrong about his circumstance! But he couldn't see it because he wasn't thinking right! Our thought life is where our life goes from bad to worse OR it goes from bad to taking it to the Lord in prayer and trusting HIM to intervene! It all depends on our mindset.

Things were about to shape up around Elijah. He had moved several miles away from the tree in the wilderness but it really was moving from one place of defeat to another and not just a change of scenery. It was also a place of defeat because Elijah saw his life on hold. He was moving about but not in his purpose. Defeat had taken over. His hope was depleted. He needed new direction to regain a better perspective for his life!

God knew that and He paid Elijah this visit to do that for him. He told Elijah to "Go out, and stand on the mountain before the Lord." Let me say, that when God interrupts our self loathing or self pity, we should be on our toes to pay attention. He does this for a reason. He is not here to play games. He comes to take us out of the dejected state we are in and turn the corner on it.

Elijah did as God directed and then amazing things began to happen! God passed by and then a strong wind tore in the mountains and broke the rocks in pieces. After that, there was an earthquake, followed by a fire. The Scripture tells us that God was not in the strong wind, or the earthquake, or the fire. God didn't speak to Elijah through these spectacular events that were going on around His prophet even though they definitely got his attention! This happens to us all. We can easily be distracted by outside forces that seek to influence our decision making. We live in a world that "quiet" is a precious commodity. There are so many different sounds going on *around* us and there are so many voices, so much *noise* and at times, it can be threatening, foreboding, and detrimental to our well-being. Perhaps Elijah felt this way on that mountain that day.

But that was not the only sound Elijah heard. He also heard a still small voice from God. When he heard that small voice from a big God, no one had to tell him Who it was. And so it is, when God speaks to your heart, you will know that you have heard from the Lord. It will be a sound like no other! And He will get to the heart of the matter with us, as He did with Elijah. Once again, the Lord asked Elijah the same question as He did earlier "What are you doing here, Elijah?" These words were not words of sympathy. It was direct and to the point. It required an answer.

Elijah's response to the Lord was all about how he had served the Lord with great zeal but *Your* people have let you down, they aren't living right, they treat me terrible. He felt so defeated! And to top it off: there is a threat made on his life. His response has all the earmarks of "I'm the best you got, Lord – so help me out in the midst of all this!"

This was no surprise to God but we all like to tell the Lord how awful things are for us, don't we! AND how He should really appreciate how wonderful we are and all we do for Him! The Lord Jesus had something to say along these lines in Luke 17: 7-10. In the context of these verses, Jesus was speaking to the disciples that however we serve the Lord is not for us to be thanked for it, but that we do it to honor Him, in a holy obligation for all He has done for us. It is our duty!

Elijah had a momentary defeated outlook because He was concentrating on how awful things had turned out for him after having served the Lord so faithfully. Well, we sympathize because we all feel that way on some level at times and we want the Lord to see things our way and come into agreement with our pitiful outlook. That will not happen, nor did it not happen for Elijah!

God's response was not to pat him on the shoulder and commiserate with him. God doesn't waste time feeling sorry for us. Neither does He want us to do that either! That gets us NO WHERE. Instead of God joining in with Elijah's sad-sack outlook, the Lord gave Elijah specific instructions for his *next mission* that had 3 phases to it! What a powerful word to Elijah!

God did not want Elijah to waste his time on his sorrows, on what might have been, or why that Jezebel hated him so! He did not want Elijah to stay on that mountain top, living holed up in a cave! Elijah had a decision to make. He had to follow God in the direction He gave him or miss out on all that God had for him in his future! It was as if God was saying to Elijah: 'No more excuses! Get out of your comfort zone and follow Me! Do not let fear control you!'

Sometimes God allows things to become uncomfortable for us to root us out of our sad sack and get on with life and with His agenda for our lives. Too often we are willing to be satisfied with a few rocks in a cave when the Lord has diamonds for us beyond the valley.

Life has its risks since we live in a fallen world. That should not interfere with making every effort to make it as wonderful as we possibly can while we are on this side of heaven. It will not happen holed up in our lofty tower or secret world, apart from those who are unkind, unthankful, unloving – even those who bear ill-will toward us. GOD is bigger than that! He will keep us and bless us regardless if they love us or not! Take my word on that.

We all realize that life may include defeat at times but *accepting* defeat is one thing and *living* with it day in and day out is another. How much better it would be to write it in the history book as over and done and begin an entirely new chapter entitled 'Better Things Coming My Way'! The next mission in life is in your future, not your past!

Think of the possibilities we could have if we listen to God's direction that He wants to give to us, which means *we need to* be quiet enough to listen. Prayer isn't only about us talking to the Lord. We need to have a quiet place of prayer where we can share our concerns with the Heavenly Father AND also be quiet enough to hear His direction for us. He will confirm the direction He gives.

God wants to change our direction, our mindset, our perception of who we are personally in the natural realm, to who we are in Him, not what someone else says! If you haven't asked the Lord to give you the direction you need, then I invite you to do so. Perhaps you have never prayed before or it has been a long time since you did. I encourage you to take the initiative to do so. Prayer isn't complicated when it comes from our heart. You just might be surprised with how things develop. A fresh start is just ahead when Hope gives us a turnaround from all our defeat!

> *"The Steps of a Good Man are ordered of the Lord, and He delights in his way. Though he fall, he shall not be utterly cast down; for the Lord upholds him with His Hand."*
>
> *Psalm 37: 23-24*

STAY THE COURSE COLLECTION WITH A HOPE-filled Perspective

First of all, I will speak from experience.

Life comes down to choices. Here are just a few to consider.

1. If I let myself only focus on what I perceive as wrong about my life, I can become discouraged, even overwhelmed by things such as: when I have worked and waited and anticipated the changes I really wanted to see come about **but** they do not happen as fast as I like; or I can't get the support I need and its "I" this or "me" that. Very little is going to change at this point! Circumstances may decline to the point that we allow ourselves to make excuses to others, but mostly to ourselves. If we continue in that mindset, we will only continue to flounder. It is no wonder we become gloomy! I understand the feeling. The truth is: our thought life can affect us in more ways than one.

Progress will come to a snail's pace. No one wants that! It helps to stop and take a reality check and make a real effort to *choose* a different perspective and ask the Lord for strength to make the necessary changes.

Consider this:

I can look at my life realistically and determine what I, myself, need to work on, those things I am capable of doing, if nothing more than organizing my office which I consider a great accomplishment! It *proves to myself* that I am preparing for something more. When I implement those changes for the better – without complaining - but with the hope that this will make a difference in my life and in the lives of those I care about. It is my choice. We always have a choice.

2. If I concentrate on others and how my life experience doesn't measure up to theirs, I can feel like a failure. It can be discouraging. Don't tell me you haven't done this! It is just human nature at times to feel this way. Confidentially, any thought that we need to measure up to someone else is an unrealistic and unwarranted idea. How much better it would be if we strived to live our best life and avoid comparisons. It is simply a waste of precious time.

The reality is, every person has a different life experience. The most important thing is our own approach to the blessings we individually have and be thankful for them and use the talents and gifts the Lord has blessed us with to benefit others in whatever form that might take.

Let me introduce you to a great example of this – my Mother. She was such a special lady. She was her own person. She worked all her life until she just had to retire. She did not consider herself well educated but she was one of the smartest women I know. One of her gifts was in knowing how to relate to people. She supervised several women in a business that was owned by a man. When she retired her boss called her to please come back to work! Things just went better when she was there! (She declined.) She was gifted with patience and a strong work ethic. Perhaps one of the most admirable qualities she had was to show people respect; to never look down on anyone including those she supervised. Especially them. They all missed her when she retired. Mother was successful because she used the mind and heart the Lord gave her to instruct people but never belittle them, and to be patient with them. She didn't waste time on what she did not have. She focused on what she did have and used that to help others move forward in life. She inspired hope and that is something we all can do! The world needs more people like her who put a smile on people's faces and the knowledge that she cared for them.

3. If I look at circumstances which I have no power to change BUT instead <u>I change</u> <u>my way of thinking</u> (which is critically important) and determine to believe that the Lord has a better plan for my life and as He helps me to understand that plan, <u>then</u> I embrace it and determine to work toward it! Then and only then will new purpose take over and Hope fills my heart again and my joy is full. It is my choice.

4. Choosing Hope is so much better than choosing to let defeat dominate my life. And it really is a choice. I realize that circumstances have a way of looming rather large over our lives at times. We do not have to *loom* with them!

If the circumstances cannot change, then perhaps the change needs to take place in *us*! Ok, be honest! I know I am not the only one that has had to do this. I have made it a matter of prayer in my life more than once to ask the Lord to help me to change whatever I need to in order to get beyond the awful mess I was facing. He has never failed to show me the way. I had to make that decision to ask for help and then follow through on the direction I receive. It is my choice but it comes down to which do we want the most – to soothe our disappointment and hurt feelings OR take whatever steps necessary to get beyond it and live a joyful and hope-filled life! I know which one I want! How about YOU?

5. If I had to guess the most common reason that we humans feel defeated at times - would be the "nuisance" desire for perfection in ourselves and especially in others. That expectation is a waste of time because it is unattainable. It simply does not exist on any level <u>on</u> <u>this</u> <u>planet</u>!

How much healthier our lives would be if we let go of the need for perfection from anyone and everyone.

Everyone – including you – will disappoint someone, at some time. Let's forgive and love one another anyway. We can live happier that way. We are only human, people. We need one another.

6. Wouldn't life be a more pleasant life experience if we extended more grace to each other and not to just those we love and who love us? Don't roll your eyes....someone extended grace to you when you were at your worst. Now, extend it to others that need it.

7. Our thought life can be our best friend or our worst enemy. Our thoughts can see all the reasons to NOT try. It is our choice to say no to those self-defeating thoughts and press on with all our might and do it. It can be the turning point for the *rest* of our life. A hopeful mindset - with corresponding actions - is better than a defeated one any day!

8. A detrimental outlook can be the cause of sinking a ship – it is always looking downward and gets everyone off course – which could be fatal!

How much better it would be if we made a quality decision to use our talents and capabilities to pivot people in a better direction, thereby making a positive difference in their lives.

With each day we can determine to hope for the best and then make every effort to do the best we can.

Some days may be steady as we go and some days may be full throttle. Consider each day we are given to be another chance to live more wisely.

9. An attitude of hope helps keep our perspective brighter, not allowing our circumstances to control us.

10. Hope encourages us and enables us to encourage others. It isn't about bubbling *'up and over'* others but by lifting their spirit through reminding them that they matter to you and to God and His love for them and His good plan for their life is still in force.

11. Learning from our mistakes is the easiest and the hardest way to learn. Easiest because we know all the facts and the hardest because we. know. all. the. facts! If we refuse to learn from it, it will be a roadblock to seeing positive change come about in our lives! And it probably means more of the same will keep happening. Which will result in us only spinning our wheels, wasting time, energy and effort. It stands to reason then that if we go ahead and bite the bullet and accept responsibility and determine to do better <u>and DO IT</u> then our lives can begin to see a real difference and *make* a real difference.

Learning from our mistakes is proof that Hope is winning in our life and defeat has lost. We are making better choices!

12. It is wisdom to make peace with your past. It is over, it is behind you. Don't re-hash it. There is no re-do for the past. Let it stay there. (Someone needs to put this on their refrigerator!)

Hope does not live with guilt or resentment for what others or yourself did or did not do because both will crowd out Hope! Let it be over.

13. You may have dropped the ball and lost the game. You blame yourself and so do others.

Instead, pick up the ball – OR – get a new one and pitch again!

Your best game is ahead of you when you are packing Hope!

14. Status quo is where many people are. How much better it is when we aim higher. That will happen when we draw closer to the Lord.

Our lives will never be Status quo when we make that a lifelong pursuit.

15. This is for anyone that feels it fits your life circumstance:

The thing that hurt you the most, that you thought you would never recover from:

It did not take you out as you thought it would! You have survived FOR A REASON!

You may have tried to shrug it off to others as unimportant, that it doesn't really matter.

But the Lord knows. And He understands and He cares. He knows the disappointment is real – in yourself and in those you trusted. The answer is found in HOPE. Because hope will take you BEYOND it ALL, if you will let it.

Ask the Lord for Hope to come alive in your heart so that you can see life differently and realize there is more to life than loss and failure. You can once again have a greater sense of purpose than you imagined! It can only happen when you leave the baggage of the past behind.

AND don't go back to reclaim it! And then that thing that hurt you so badly – whether it was others or a self-inflicted wound - will become a steppingstone that propels you in a different direction for your life. It may take a while but you will see how your experience can become a testimony that touches the lives of others! HOPE is the starting point. Take it. There is a verse in Hebrews 6 verse 19 that speaks of Hope as an anchor. This is based on 2 factors found in verses 17-18 that tell us there are two things that we can be confident of as a person of faith in God. Those two things are God's unchanging nature and His unchanging Word. People can be fickle. It's true. God is not like people!

When we trust in the Lord, our confidence is never misplaced. Rather, our hope is firmly anchored in Him, and in His Word. An anchor can look good, look strong but it is only beneficial because of the stronger base to which it is connected. As people of faith in Christ, our hope is linked to the two unchangeable truths that He will not change nor will His Word. That is a guarantee that we will not sink! We will rise!

On a personal note, in January of 2023 on the morning of the 26th, I got up at 6 a.m. to get started on my day. My devotional time comes first. At that particular time, my mind became bombarded with thoughts of past failures. It happened all of a sudden! It was obvious the source of these thoughts. I needed to get control before my entire day was ruined! I had help. I sat down on the sofa in our living room and a sweet presence came over me. You may not believe this, but I know the truth of my experience. The greatest voice, the Lord, spoke to my heart this time to tell me "You are moving forward. Don't look back." This gave me such joy and encouraged my faith and inspired hope within me that my failures were indeed in the past, It was up to me to leave them there. The Lord was moving me forward without the weight of the past. He has proven those words to me. Five months later, the turning point came.

16. I have found that circumstances have great power in that they can accomplish more than one thing in our lives. Let me list a few: Our circumstances can harden us or make us pliable; purify us or contaminate us; define us negatively or positively; propel us or hinder us; strengthen us or weaken us; toughen us or soften us; teach us, develop us, empower us, fulfill us or diminish us and rob us. Our circumstances have great ability, but they cannot take *our ability* in how we respond! We do that all by ourselves. We have the ability to make the choice even when faced with the meanest of all circumstances to choose to respond in faith and hope in God that even though we have been shaken, He has not. He will sustain us through it all to be better, stronger, kinder, wiser and more compassionate of others.

"Jesus Christ is the same yesterday, today and forever."

Hebrews 13: 8

EPILOGUE

In closing, I want to share with you a lovely verse from Psalm 42: 11 where the writer asks a question of himself and then he realizes the answer. It reads:

> *"Why are you cast down, O my soul? And why are you disquieted within me? Hope in God; for I shall yet praise Him, the help of my countenance and my God."*

This verse reveals the heart of a man who was distraught due to his circumstances. He felt God had forgotten him; his enemies taunted him. He felt so defeated. But he did not stay that way. I believe Hope must have reminded him of the goodness and faithfulness of the Lord. He surely must have looked up at that moment and corrected his thinking and made a quality decision to once again, trust in the Lord, to hope in His God and to continue to praise Him for all the things He had done for him in the past and that He would not fail to help him now.

I do not know where you are on your life's journey. You may be on top of the world or you may feel overwhelmed by defeat. Allow me to remind you of God's goodness and His infinite love for you. Let Hope arise in your heart even though everything seems to shout defeat and *trust* that God will lead you to triumph! The word Hope means expectation, to look hopefully in a particular direction. Look up to the Lord and He will help you.

Blessings to you and those you love,

Myra Woodbridge
www.myrawoodbridge - author
Facebook: The Path Forward – Myra Woodbridge

ENDORSEMENTS

"I read The Path Forward and it speaks to the heart and soul of anyone searching for a deeper relationship with Christ. Myra shares her and Terry's experience with the struggles we all have but sometimes are reluctant to share. Most importantly she gives God all the praise and glory for the season they went through. The Path Forward is an easy-to-read book that can be shared with anyone regardless of their age. Myra outlines several struggles that each reader can relate to. Mine was number 11! (under Stay the Course section) Read it and find yours. I can't wait until "Hope Beyond Defeat" is published."

Diane Bentley

Mount Holly Church Member

"I truly enjoyed "The Path Forward." It is beautifully written, with deep insight of God's Word and promises. Her personal experiences and faith are so heartfelt and inspiring."

Kim Brown

"The Path Forward touched my heart. Mrs. Woodbridge has a gift of teaching. Her knowledge and deep understanding of the Bible are most valuable."

Cindy

REMEMBER

I have shared with you testimonies of the goodness of God at work in the lives of people who love Him with all their heart. I hope it has ministered to you. God is bigger than any disappointment or failure or betrayal that you have experienced in your life too. I want you to remember that His goodness has nothing to do with the circumstances you face in this life. The Lord's love never fades. Circumstances come and go just as people may, but His love is permanent. Whatever your circumstances, whatever area of defeat you may have in your life, whatever burdens you have today, remember that He cares for you. He is only a prayer away. He can change circumstances and people. Let Hope take over in your heart and see defeat take a back seat permanently.

Your future awaits you!

If you do not know the reality of your sins being forgiven and being assured of going to heaven after this life is passed, please call on the Lord today. Simply ask Him to forgive you and commit your life to Him. Study His Word and live by it and your life will have a peace and joy that you never dreamed possible. A new season awaits you in Christ!